Whittling & Wood Carving

H. Hoppe

 STERLING PUBLISHING CO., INC.
NEW YORK

THE OAK TREE PRESS, Ltd., London and Sydney
SAUNDERS OF TORONTO, Ltd., Don Mills, Canada

Little Craft Book Series

Translated by Eric Greweldinger

Fifth Printing, 1973
Copyright © 1969 by Sterling Publishing Co., Inc.
419 Park Avenue South, New York, N.Y. 10016
Simultaneously published and Copyright © 1969 in Canada
by Saunders of Toronto, Ltd., Don Mills, Ontario
British edition published by Oak Tree Press Co., Ltd., Nassau, Bahamas
Distributed in Australia and New Zealand by Oak Tree Press Co., Ltd.,
P.O. Box 34, Brickfield Hill, Sydney 2000, N.S.W.
Distributed in the United Kingdom and elsewhere in the British Commonwealth
by Ward Lock Ltd., 116 Baker Street, London W 1
The original edition was published in Germany under the title
"Schnitzen in Holz" © 1966 by Verlag Frech, Stuttgart-Botnang, Germany.
Manufactured in the United States of America
All rights reserved
Library of Congress Catalog Card No.: 69-19488
ISBN 0-8069-5126-5   U.K. 7061 2156 2
5127-3

Contents

Before You Begin

Illus. 1. Characteristics of the wood, such as its grain, contribute to the effect of the work. Whether to smooth the wood, as in this figure, or to leave it with tool marks is a personal choice.

The main purpose of this book is to acquaint you with the technical aspects of wood carving. When you make a design for a wood carving, you must know the wood and master the carving technique. Each material has its own limits and possibilities. Wood is different from metal, stone or clay. Moreover, the many varieties of wood have different characteristics and should be worked in different ways. The texture, grain and color of the wood will all be studied later in this book, and whether you are interested in simple chip carving or in sculpturing figures out of wood, you will be prepared when you make your design.

In fact, a distinction is sometimes made between carvers who ornament objects, like furniture and bowls, and wood sculptors, who chisel a fully three-dimensional work from a block of wood. But many persons master both techniques, and the instructions in this book should guide you from ornamental carving to sculpturing in wood. Whatever carving you do, you will learn to give it your own personal touch.

(Note: The word "timber" as used in this book refers to all dressed planks of wood no matter what size or shape.)

Staff Carving

In many parts of the world, shepherds adorn their staffs by cutting rings of bark from freshly cut branches. This is probably the oldest form of wood carving as a folk art. For this project, you will find it comparatively easy to carve into a square bar of wood. All you need is the short, well-sharpened blade of a pocketknife. Birch, walnut and mahogany are good woods for this purpose. You can obtain square bars of 1 × 1 or 2 × 2 inches, cut to the length you want, from a timber-yard (lumber-yard) or a cabinetmaker.

Draw horizontal lines with a try square or a right-angle gauge on the four sides of the bar (Illus. 2, *a*). Draw diagonal and vertical lines with a ruler or by hand. You can use your hand and pencil as a scratch gauge, as shown in Illus. 2, *b*, if you draw lines which run parallel to the vertical edges.

In your design, take care to preserve bars of wood between the horizontal cuts; otherwise, the corners can

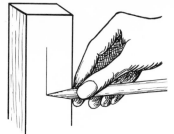

Illus. 2b (above). Use hand and pencil as scratch gauge.

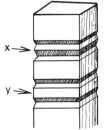

Illus. 3 (right). Leave bars of wood (y) between cuts. If you do not (x), the corners may break.

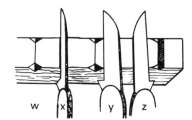

Illus. 4. Cut notches (w) if wood is hard. Make perpendicular cut (x), then two oblique ones (y and z).

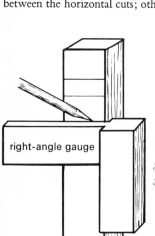

right-angle gauge

Illus. 2a. Draw horizontal guidelines with a right-angle gauge.

easily crack off (Illus. 3). If you carve an often used utensil, for instance a letter opener, first round off the four edges and only then start carving.

Horizontal cuts are made by dividing the desired width in half and cutting along the dividing line with the pocketknife perpendicular to the wood. Then, with the knife held at an angle, you cut toward the bottom of the dividing line from both sides of it (see Illus. 4). If the wood is hard, cut small notches at the edges of the bar as shown by *w*.

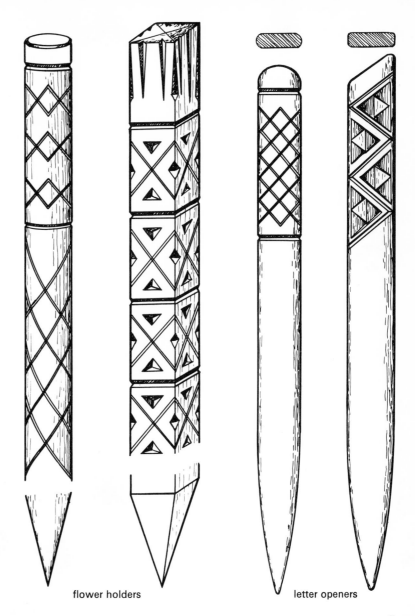

Illus. 5. Use the principles of staff carving to make rods for supporting flowers and to make letter openers.

flower holders   letter openers

7

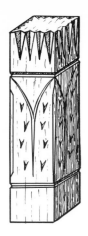

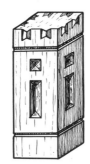

Illus. 6. Chess pieces are created by carving the bar, dividing it into sections and adding details. At the left are three castles; at the right are three views of a knight piece.

Sets of chess pieces can be made in this way. You should choose a heavy wood, as the pieces must be stable, or you can drill a hole in the base and tap some lead into it. For the dark pieces, you can use mahogany or walnut, and for the light ones, you can use birch or maple. After the whole bar has been carved, you saw off the individual pieces in a mitre box, and further refinements may be added.

Carved bars are also used as a support for plants. For this purpose, you can use round bars, which you purchase as dowelling wood in timber-yards or hardware shops. You can obtain a beautiful effect by using branches of hazel wood; the dark color of the bark and the light color of the wood result in a nice contrast. Be careful not to apply an intricate design to a support for flowering potted plants; the flowers—and not the supports—are most important, and the design should be simple.

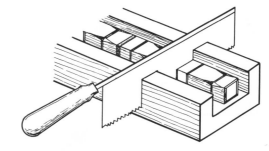

Illus. 7. Divide the carved bar into sections with a mitre box and saw.

Chip Carving

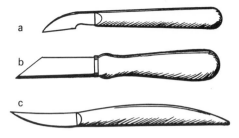

Illus. 8. Chip-carving knives: (a) regular, (b) for deeper, larger cuts, (c) for straight and curved lines.

This is an ancient technique which has been preserved through the centuries. Based on a few elementary designs, ornaments such as friezes, mouldings, and rosettes are executed in this way.

Carving knives for chip carving have a short blade as they are held with one hand only, in contrast to the tools for wood sculpture. You only need three knives for your work (Illus. 8). These can be purchased in most hardware shops or in special handicraft shops. Of course, you can also use your pocketknife as well, using the short blade, which you should have ground to a point by an expert. Have the back of the blade ground half-round. Wrap the connection between blade and handle with insulating tape. This will protect the skin of your index finger.

For chip carving, you mainly cut with the point of your knife, which therefore must be kept very sharp. The best woods for chip carving are woods without a strong grain effect, as the grain would detract too much from the design. For use with knives, only soft woods are suitable (see chapter on wood), but you can use the same technique on medium-hard woods if you use a mallet and chisel (see chapter on tools).

The best way to draw the design on the wood is by using your try square, a compass and a ruler. If you cannot do this, trace the design with graphite paper on light woods and with carbon paper on darker woods. A pencil that is well sharpened and has a fairly hard lead is best suited to this purpose. Remnants of graphite lines can be erased after carving; remove lines of carbon with fine sandpaper. But ideally you should work in such a way that there will be no traces left after carving.

How to draw your first exercise is shown by Illus. 9. First draw two horizontal lines with your try square to form a space $\frac{3}{16}$ of an inch in width, and then divide the horizontal space vertically in distances of $\frac{3}{8}$ inches. Also draw the diagonal lines shown in rectangle *b*. Now carve the diagonal lines on the left and right sides with your knife "a." Hold your knife vertically. The tops of the triangles should be carved deeply.

With the third cut, shown in rectangles *e* and *f*, you hold your knife rather flat and carve out the little triangle from the right to the left. This last cut is more difficult than the diagonal ones. After some trying, you will succeed in making the cuts in a "clean" way. Your knife must be so sharp that the freshly cut surface of the wood has a gloss. For the diagonal cuts you may hold your knife as a fountain pen; the index finger then exerts pressure from above. Try until you find the best way for *you* to hold your knife (see next page).

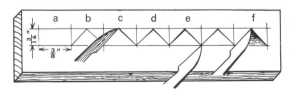

Illus. 9. Draw your design first. Follow steps in text.

Illus. 10. Grip knife firmly. Carve with the grain.

For safety, clamp the board to a worktable and keep both hands behind the cutting tool. When it is necessary to turn the work in another direction, either shift your position, or reclamp the board. By turning the board, you can cut with the grain or across it, instead of against it. (See "Wood.") Never cut toward your body. Illus. 11 shows a finished row of triangles. Combining two such rows results in a row of lozenges, which may be further decorated by additional incisions in the lozenges (Illus. 11, *b*). You can obtain different effects by drawing out the lozenges or compressing them. These few examples illustrate some of the variety of forms that can be obtained by using this single elementary design.

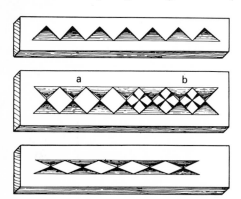

Illus. 11. (top) Row of triangles, (middle) two facing rows create lozenges (a), (bottom) expanded lozenges.

If you want to obtain deeper and larger cuts, you work with the knives "a" and "b." Start again by drawing the horizontal lines and dividing them vertically, but increase the measures (Illus. 12). Then draw the triangles, which you divide as shown by the dotted lines in *b*. Place your knife in the middle of the triangle and cut along the three dividing lines to the corners. You may hold the knife in a pen grip if you are using very soft wood; for harder wood, hold the knife in your fist (Illus. 13). The cutting out of the triangles is shown in Illus. 12, *c* to *f*; you slice out each of the three chips by cutting along the perimeter. Diamond-shaped cutouts are made the same way, only you divide the diamond into fourths instead of thirds (Illus. 13).

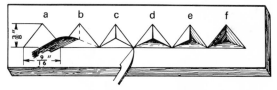

Illus. 12. For larger and deeper cuts, divide triangle.

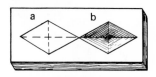

Illus. 13. Use dagger grip for hard wood. Divide diamond-shape into quarters (a), then carve as usual (b).

Straight lines are cut with your knife "c" or with your pocketknife. Hold the knife in such a way that the blade penetrates the wood for its maximum length; this

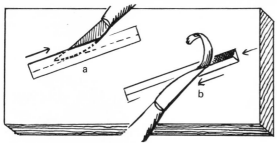

Illus. 14. For straight lines, make two oblique cuts (a and b) that meet in the middle of the desired width.

makes it easier to cut straight lines. Instead of having the blade perpendicular to the wood, you hold it at an angle. After some exercise, you will succeed in carving a line with two oblique cuts. The width and depth of the cuts depend on the desired effect. Deep cuts cause deep shadows and give more effect. Illus. 14 shows lines that have been cut diagonally across the grain.

Curved lines are cut with a knife that is as narrow and as pointed as possible. The knife is held more upright than for straight lines. Curved lines are often carved wider and deeper in the middle, with both ends narrow. This results in a nice effect. You may also carve the lines with a sharp parting tool (see "Tools"). The illustrations show examples of curved lines.

Illus. 16. Use curved lines alone or with other cuts.

A very well-known design is a rosette divided into six segments (Illus. 17). For this, you start by dividing the circumference with a middle line through the circle. Place your compass in point 1 at the end of the middle line and find points 3 and 5 by setting the compass to equal the radius. Do the same with the compass set in point 2 to find points 4 and 6. Then halve the six parts and draw the points of the six-pointed star.

Illus. 15. Very pointed knife cuts curved lines best.

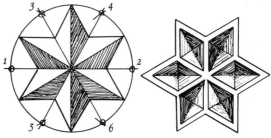

Illus. 17. Rosette design is drawn with compass.

11

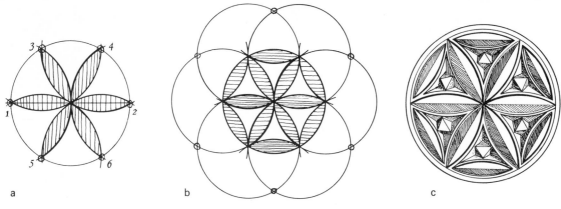

a   b   c

Illus. 18. A compass is also used for this leaf design. Follow the instructions in the text very closely.

The six stylized leaves in Illus. 18 have been drawn with the compass only. Place the compass successively in points 1 and 2 and draw two half-circles (from point 1 to 6 and from point 2 to 5). Then place the compass in points 3, 4, 5 and 6 for drawing the leaves.

The space between the leaves and the circumference may be filled by drawing the same form six times on the circumference. You find the six intersections by drawing six full circles (Illus. 18, *b*), made by placing the compass point at each of the numbered points. This decoration is very old. Of course, you may use many other designs for dividing stars and rosettes.

Chip-carved ornaments consist of basic geometric designs (triangle, square, circle, etc.). Therefore, if you copy natural forms, you must simplify them. The illustrated book ends show this.

Illus. 19. Chip-carving can ornament useful objects such as book ends, but keep design of natural forms simple.

Veneer Carving

The effect of chip carving may be enhanced by applying color. By painting the carved-out lines you increase their shadow-effect. You can also paint the whole surface of the wood before carving it, and in that way obtain more contrast after the carving has been done. But applying paint means that the very beauty of the wood—its structure and own color—is lost, at least partly. Therefore, you should apply paint as an exception only.

You can, however, attain a similar contrasting effect of color without losing the proper beauty of the wood by veneer carving. You apply a veneer, a thin layer of high-grade wood, to a board and carve the veneer. Veneer carving offers excellent possibilities and the work is not difficult.

Glue a dark veneer on a light-colored plank with wood cement or special veneering glue. Then you draw and carve as you did before. You may, of course, also affix light-colored veneer to a dark underground; this depends on your design. For a design consisting mainly of lines, dark on light is preferable. The carved lines then appear light. You must take into consideration that light lines on a dark background seem thinner than dark lines on a light background.

For larger works, you can use furniture veneer (mahogany, walnut, etc.), but this is too thick for small works. You can still use furniture veneer, which is $\frac{1}{16}$ of an inch thick, if you carefully plane and polish it after cementing it on to the wood. It should be well cleaned after polishing to prevent your knives from becoming dull.

For small pieces, you can also use a type of wall-covering which consists of very thin wood veneer glued on paper. After soaking this material for about one hour with a wet cloth, you can separate the veneer from the paper. Some plywood companies also manufacture paper-thin veneer, 1/85 of an inch thick, which has been reinforced by paper or cloth on its back. You

light veneer   dark board   dark veneer   light board   birch veneer over mahogany

Illus. 20. Veneer (thin wood) is glued to a board and parts are carved away in a design. Other tools are needed.

13

Illus. 21. Birds were carved from dark veneer on a light background, which shows in design after veneer is cut away.

Illus. 22. Horses are also of dark veneer. Gouges are used to cut away background.

cannot separate the veneer, as it is too thin. This veneer, glued on, is sometimes used for small work and for display material, but requires expert handling.

Large, solid boards warp. Therefore you should use plywood if you make larger objects, cementing one or two layers of veneer on to it, depending on whether or not you can use the surface of your plywood board as a background for the design. You cannot use the plywood surface if it is of low-grade and blemished.

In typical chip carving, the effect is a result of the shadows cast by the cuts and lines. In veneer carving, the effect is obtained by the contrasting colors of the woods. The results are similar to prints made from lino-blocks and woodcuts.

For most of the work shown in the illustrations, you will need more tools than your three knives. To carve out the background properly, you will need chisels and gouges, tools which will be discussed on the next pages. A bent parting tool and small curved gouges come in handy for carving the lines.

Tools and Work Place

Now that you have done some work with wood, you will want to know more about tools. For chip carving, you do not need more than the three knives already discussed. To carve bowls and boards, you will need some cutting tools called chisels, which are flat, and gouges, which are curved. These are available in widths from $\frac{1}{8}$ to 2 inches. If you intend to make various types of objects, you should purchase a set of tools composed by experts.

From the illustrated tools you can see there is a wide variety from which to choose (Illus. 23). The line next to each tool indicates the cut it makes. A gouge with a deep curvature is called a fluting tool. Shanks may be straight or bent. As you proceed, you will complete your collection by selecting the tools most suited to your needs. A sculptor who works in wood will have as many as 50 to 70 tools.

Chisels are fundamental instruments. They have straight cutting edges and function in two ways: the sharp cutting edge cuts into and separates the wood along a specific path, while the bevel and thickness of the chisel serve as wedges and force the wood apart. The cutting and splitting may occur simultaneously or one may rapidly follow the other. The smaller the wedge-angle or bevel on the chisel, the easier will be the carving.

Gouges are tools with curved cutting edges. There are many varieties of them. Gouges with bent shanks are used for deep cutting. You will find out which tools to use through experience.

You must keep your tools clean and as sharp as razors. When not in use, you can protect them by lightly oiling them and keeping them in a dry place.

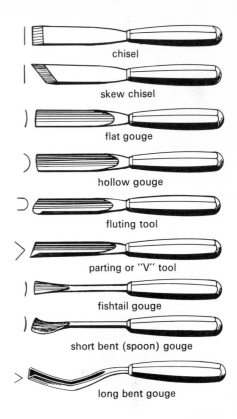

chisel

skew chisel

flat gouge

hollow gouge

fluting tool

parting or "V" tool

fishtail gouge

short bent (spoon) gouge

long bent gouge

Illus. 23. Various chisels and gouges are needed for cutting deeply into the wood and carving out forms.

Never keep more tools on your worktable than those you need for the work in progress. Hang the others on a wall rack. Too many tools on your worktable only delay the choice of a tool. If you take your tools to other places, use a large piece of soft, clean cloth, with partitions for the different tools, which you can roll up and carry with you. In this way, you can protect the cutting edges when the instruments are not in use.

Besides chisels and gouges, you need wooden forms called mallets (Illus. 24), which are used as hammers. For blocking out initial masses of wood, you use a heavy mallet with a fairly large instrument. As carving progresses, you use flat chisels and small gouges with lighter mallets. For sawing you need a ripsaw and a crosscut saw for large cuts and a fret saw, coping saw or powered jigsaw for scroll-like cuts.

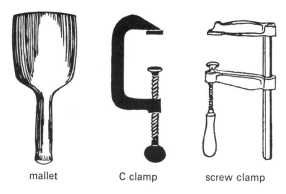

mallet   C clamp   screw clamp

Illus. 24. Mallet is for hammering; clamps hold work.

Other tools used are: rasps and files for abrasive action; compasses, calipers, and a try square for measuring and ruling; a vise, screw clamps or C clamps, and a long screw (bench screw) for holding your work steady; and a punctuating device for point-by-point measuring.

As a worktable, wood carvers use a carving bench, which is similar to a carpenter's bench, only it is higher and has just one vise. You can use a sturdy table, which should be as heavy as possible. It should be high enough so that you can work in a standing position.

For incised carving, a place at a window will do; for other types of carving you need a well-lit workshop, if possible with natural light coming from the north. Artificial light should light the whole room; a ceiling

light is preferred. In addition, you will need an adjustable light at your worktable. The size of your workshop depends on the type of work you intend to do.

Keeping your chisels and gouges sharp is essential. Sharpen these tools first on a grindstone. However, this is not for beginners and you should let the shop where you buy your tools sharpen them. Later you can take your tools to a professional wood carver and ask for a practical demonstration. The instruments are sharpened or ground on only one side. The reverse side is best kept perfectly flat, and the cutting edges should be kept even and straight.

If the edge of an instrument becomes chipped, the nicks can be ground off on a grindstone at an angle of

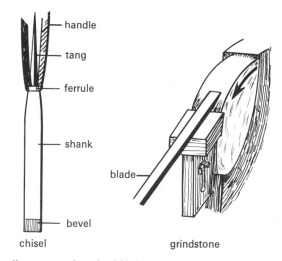

handle

tang

ferrule

shank

blade—

bevel

chisel   grindstone

Illus. 25. Bevel on chisel blade is ground on a stone.

from $10°$ to $15°$. If the angle is too small, the instrument will not remain sharp and will easily become nicked. As a simple rule, the length of the bevel should be two times the thickness of the blade (Illus. 26).

16

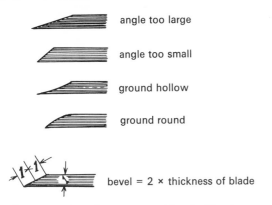

angle too large

angle too small

ground hollow

ground round

bevel = 2 × thickness of blade

Illus. 26. Study angle, evenness and length of bevel.

After it has been ground, an instrument must be whetted on an oilstone, with the chisel held at the same angle as the bevel. Both coarse and fine oilstones are generally used for sharpening flat chisels. The first sharpening is done on Carborundum or India stones; the final edge is on Arkansas or Washita. A few drops of machine oil placed on the stone surface will serve as a lubricant. Hold the chisel with the bevelled end lying flat on the stone and, when this is at the correct angle, grasp the tool firmly with both hands and then move the tool back and forth (Illus. 27). The stone should be held in place by wood fastened to the table. As you move the chisel away from you, exert a gentle pressure. And as you draw it toward you, ease the pressure. A spiral motion, utilizing a large area of the oilstone, is recommended.

A burr, or rough edge, will have formed on the opposite side of the chisel. Remove this by drawing the chisel, flat side down, several times across each of the oilstones.

With gouges, the sharpening method is sometimes reversed. The gouge is held stationary and the stone is moved so that it contacts all parts of the bevel. Specially shaped slipstones are employed (Illus. 28). The burr is removed by rubbing the curve of the slipstone against the inside of the gouge.

Finally, the instruments can be made razor-sharp by stropping them on a leather strop (as used for razors) or on a piece of hardwood. All oil must be wiped off the tool first. In all cases, the length of the bevel on the cutting end of the tools should be retained, and particular care should be exercised, during the sharpening process, not to shorten the bevel.

You should strop your instruments often and whet them on stones whenever they become blunt. Have them ground only when they become notched.

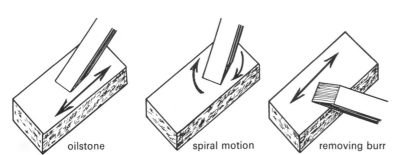

oilstone · spiral motion · removing burr

Illus. 27. After being ground, chisel bevel must be sharpened on an oilstone.

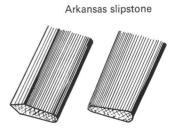

Arkansas slipstone

Illus. 28. Use slipstones for gouges.

17

Wood: Characteristics and Varieties

Knowing the characteristics of wood will help you to select the right type of wood for your work and to proceed properly. This chapter will be a guide for you.

Illus. 29 shows a crosscut of a log. The rings are caused by the tree's annual growth. The most recently grown year-rings form the sapwood, which contains active, living cells in contrast to the older year-rings, the heartwood, which has inactive cells. The growth of the year-rings is one factor in determining the grain

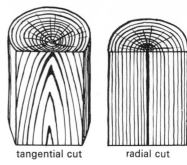

Illus. 30. *Grain you see depends on way log is cut.*

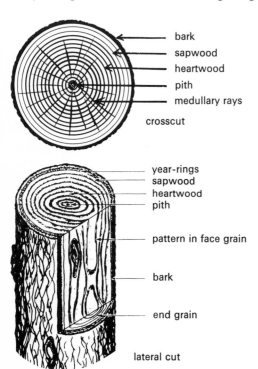

Illus. 29. *Two views of log show features of wood.*

pattern found in planks of timber. Grain is the fibrous structure of the tree. The pattern it shows on a plank is also affected by how the log is sawed (Illus. 30). Face grain on a plank runs in one direction only. End grain results from the crosscut of the log. The medullary rays, which are especially prominent in oak, radiate from the middle of the tree's trunk.

One of the significant facts you must consider is that wood is subject to shrinkage and warping. This is because of its water content. After being cut into boards and planks and being "seasoned," the water content of a log drops from 60 per cent to about 15 per cent by evaporation. Wood is seasoned either by leaving it under protection in the open air or putting it into specially heated rooms to dry. As a wood mass dries, the moisture or "cell water" in the cells slowly evaporates and a contraction takes place. If the humidity increases, the wood again absorbs water and increases in volume. This may cause undue "checking" (deep cracks are called "checks"), warping and twisting. The greatest stress or movement takes place across the grain. The movement with the grain is generally small.

Seasoning is too difficult for the beginner to attempt. You can either buy planks at a timber-yard or logs at shops that specialize in sculptors' supplies. If necessary,

18

you can glue planks together to form a block for carving. Bear in mind, however, that shrinkage varies much between the various woods. The outer year-rings are softer, they contain more water and contract more during the drying process than the inner rings. This causes the bending in lateral planks (Illus. 31). When planks are glued together this must be taken into consideration. Heartwood should be joined to heartwood and sapwood to sapwood (Illus. 32).

Planks are graded according to quality. You should select wood that has as few defects (knotholes, etc.) as possible. Get advice from your timber merchant. Use waterproof glue and clamp the planks together with furniture clamps, rope or heavy weights until dry.

Logs may develop checks even after seasoning. You can either ignore them or fill them in with wood sealers that come in putty form and harden. If you work on an unseasoned log, cover it with heavy plastic between sessions to prevent rapid drying. If possible, hollow out the middle and seal the ends with paint. Lumber from discarded furniture is also a good source of wood for carving.

The botanical use of the terms "hardwood" and "softwood" to denote whether the timber comes from broad-leafed trees or from coniferous trees has little value for the wood carver, as some so-called hardwoods are actually soft and vice versa. We will use the terms here to denote the ease with which the wood can be carved. The following is a list of some woods for carving.

Linden (basswood, lime-tree) is a fairly common softwood with a straight, close grain. It is light in weight, uniform in structure and quite easily carved. Its heartwood varies from a creamy white to a medium reddish-brown.

Walnut is one of the finest sculptural woods and requires the use of very sharp tools. Close-grained wal-

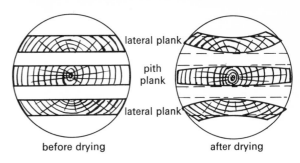

Illus. 31. Loss of water content results in warping.

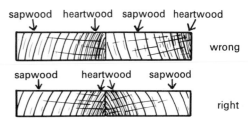

Illus. 32. When glueing planks, join ends as above.

nut, such as Italian, is the best variety for carving, as it permits a delicacy of detail. American (black) walnut is also an excellent medium-hard wood for carving purposes.

Mahogany is strong and of medium weight. It has great beauty and durability. The Philippine variety is softer than the Honduras. In the former, the natural color of the finished wood is a warm, reddish-brown. Mahogany is capable of taking a high polish. It is highly resistant to humidity and it will warp less than other woods. It is also resistant to mould and decay. African mahogany is one of the softest varieties. The wood has larger pores than American mahogany and it is luxuriously figured with stripes, mottles and swirls.

Cherry is a close-grained wood with minute pores. Though harder than walnut, it is an excellent wood for carving, as are most fruit woods. Wild cherry-wood varies from light to dark reddish-brown.

Pine—Northern white, ponderosa and sugar are all easily carved soft woods.

Redwood is slightly harder than pine, but has good texture and weathers well.

Elm is a hard, light-to-dark brown wood suitable for large carvings.

Illus. 33. The longitudinal grain of this wood stresses the horizontal direction of the fish.

Illus. 34. This fish has an upward direction, enhanced by the cone-shaped pattern of the grain.

Birch. There are many varieties of this hard and strong wood. Yellow birch and red birch are cut for timber. American canoe birch and European white birch have light, strong, close-grained wood.

Oak is a hard, tough, close-grained, durable and beautiful wood, but subject to warping and checking. The wood is resistant to insect attacks and it can be given a high polish. Oak is excellent for carving broad, strong designs. Red oak is not as good as white oak for carving. The color of oak heartwood varies from cream or yellow to a dark brown. The color of most varieties can be darkened with ammonia.

Poplar is a soft, light and durable wood which is easily carved. The heartwood varies from a light yellow to a brownish color.

Rosewoods are even-textured, smooth, scented tropical hardwoods. Brazilian rosewood, also known as palisander or jacaranda, is extremely fine, rare and expensive. Although hard and brittle, the wood can be carved. The color is dark brown, streaked with black or yellow. East Indian rosewood is a little softer and has a more purplish tinge.

Teakwood varies from a yellow to a golden brown. The wood is quite hard and strong. It has a coarse, uneven texture but can be carved readily. Teakwood is durable; it possesses an oily component that repels insects.

Boxwood is a very fine-textured, tough hardwood. It has a uniform yellow color and is good for carving details.

No material offers such a variety as wood. You should consider the ease of carving, the durability, and the effects of grain pattern together with the color when you decide on a piece of wood for your work. You can stress your design by the longitudinal stripes of the face grain on certain boards or by the cone-shaped grain pattern of other boards. (See Illus. 33 and 34.) For slender free-standing forms, you must use the wood longitudinally, not horizontally, or the piece will break.

For small works with intricate detail, choose a simple wood with little grain effect. (See Illus. 40.)

Of the coniferous woods, pine (except the yellow longleaf variety) is the best for carving, as it cuts easily and will retain details if sharp tools are used. From the broad-leafed trees, the medium-hard woods are best for the beginner. Philippine mahogany and walnut are good choices.

Ornamental Carving

Draw the design on the wood or transfer it with carbon paper and a sharp pencil. Attach the board you are going to carve to your worktable with screw clamps, using cardboard between the top of the clamp and the board to protect the wood surface (Illus. 35).

A carved ornament consists of lines and planes, and of hollow and rounded masses. Illus. 36 shows an ornament with a rounded mass in the middle and six hollow forms for leaves. These are elementary forms and are repeated with many variations in different designs. Hollow forms are carved with a gouge that is slightly smaller than the intended cut-out. Rounded forms—like grapes, pearls, etc.—are carved with a reversed chisel or gouge.

Illus. 37 shows the gouge cutting the outlines of the drawing, then carving out the background, and finally removing excess wood on the raised design. At first, carving the background will present difficulties. If you succeed in doing this neatly with clean cuts, the ornament will contrast better with the background. However, do not use sandpaper or files to finish the background.

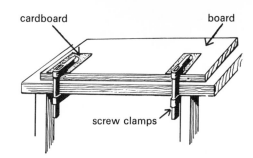

Illus. 35. Fasten board to table with screw clamps.

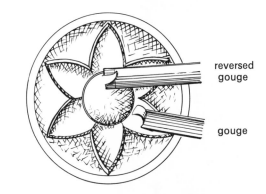

Illus. 36. Carve hollows with gouge; reverse tool to shape rounded forms as in the middle of this design.

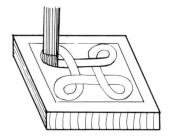
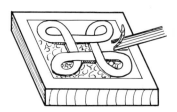
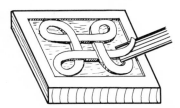

Illus. 37. First, outline drawing with vertical cuts; remove unwanted background; finish by shaping details.

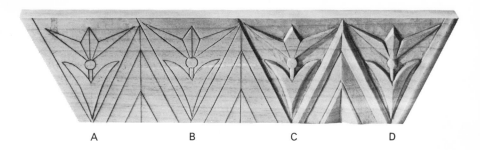

Illus. 38. Photograph demonstrates step-by-step instructions in the text.

A   B   C   D

Illus. 38 again pictures how an ornament is carved. *A* shows the drawing on the wood, *B* the carved contour lines made with the tool driven vertically into the wood. In *C*, the background has been carved out with a gouge driven at an angle. If the depth of the background is not sufficient after the first carving, you repeat the same procedure, carving out the contour lines again and then carving out the background deeper. *D* shows the finished ornament.

For the "blocking out" process (making the relief carving in rough form), you use your mallet with gouges and chisels, and for the detailed finishing you use well-stropped tools pushed by hand. (See Illus. 39 and 40, and Illus. 41, next page.)

Illus. 39. Ornamental panel was blocked out with mallet, chisels and gouges.

Illus. 40. Details were added to above panel with tools pushed by hand.

When carving, hold the tool in your left hand and push it from behind with your right hand (Illus. 41). (Naturally, if you are left-handed, you would reverse the procedure.) For making the initial cuts, hold the tool in your left hand and the mallet in your right hand. If you must carve out large masses, for instance when hollowing out a bowl, you may find it necessary to change hands. The tool and mallet should be held in a firm grip, but not too forcefully or you will soon tire. The mallet should hit the tool at a right angle (Illus. 41), and the blows should originate from your elbow, not from your shoulder.

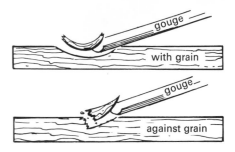

Illus. 42. Carve with the grain, not against it.

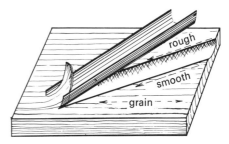

Illus. 43. You can cut diagonally across the grain.

As much as possible, carve in the direction of the wood fibres. You can tell you are carving in the correct direction if the chips come out cleanly and are not broken or jagged at the end (Illus. 42). However you cannot always carve in this direction because the design may not allow it. If you carve in a direction opposite the fibres, you are carving *against* the grain and will have to smooth the cut with one from the opposite direction. If you carve diagonally across the grain (Illus. 43), one side of the cut will be smooth and the other side rough (hatched lines). Carving is easier if you turn the tool somewhat around its axis while pushing it.

Illus. 41. Mallet should strike the tool at a right angle. When pushing tool, keep both hands behind it.

Carving Letters in Wood

The letters or characters in our alphabet are based on the so-called Antiqua, a type developed by the ancient Romans and carved in stone. Monks used it for writing during the Middle Ages, and during this period, the first small-case characters originated. In the course of centuries, many different variations have been developed from this basis. All these variations have their own characteristics, which should be taken into consideration when using them. An amateur, who intends to carve lettering in wood should start by studying this subject, on which much literature has been published.

Woods with striking grain patterns distract from the expression and lines of the characters. On the other hand, the structure of the wood can effectively enhance the type used. For inscriptions which are being placed in the open air, weather-resistant woods should be used, for instance white oak, pine (except ponderosa) and mahogany.

First make some sketches of your design. Then draw it in the size to be carved. The illustration here

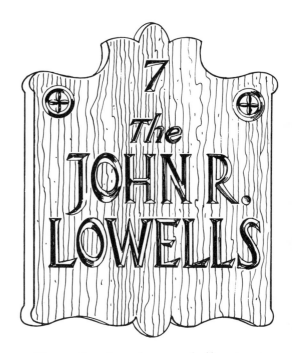

Illus. 44. Carve letters for name-and-address signpost.

LOWELLS
LOWELLS

shows that you may not maintain the same distance between the individual characters. They should be spaced in such a manner that the word forms a unity. A beginner always places vertical characters, like the M, I and N too close together and maintains too much space between the A, the L, the O, etc.

You can carve the characters fairly easily on softwood with your chip-carving knives and a parting tool, and on hardwood with your mallet, chisels and gouges. Make a vertical cut in the middle of the character and chip or chisel the wood away obliquely on either side leaving two slopes that meet in the middle. The carving of characters in high relief is more difficult. Basically, you use the same technique as you do for ornamental carving.

Bowls and Candlesticks

Illus. 45. Wooden utensils like this cup are historic.

Wooden utensils have been made throughout history and by all peoples. In museums, you will find many fine examples of folk art, often with forms that have a symbolic meaning, for instance drinking cups shaped like birds (Illus. 45). The material and artistry of the wood carver lend a unique quality to wooden bowls and plates. The beauty of the material should not be superseded by too much ornamentation.

For carving, you can use woods without much grain effect—like maple, birch, oak or American walnut—or, you can stress the shape of a bowl by using prominently-grained wood.

Draw the contours of the bowl on the surface of the wood and then clamp the piece to a worktable with two screw clamps or C clamps. For blocking out, use a large gouge driven by your mallet. Work as much with the grain as possible. To prevent damaging the inner rim of the bowl, first cautiously carve a trench with your gouge (Illus. 46, *a*). Then carve the inner edge with a rather flat gouge (Illus. 46, *b*), and from top to bottom block out the hollow form of the bowl. The finishing cuts should produce an artful, smooth effect and polish-

ing should be done only if required by the use of the bowl, for instance for a fruit bowl.

After you have made the hollow form, the round shape should be sawed out of the board with a coping saw or a jigsaw (Illus. 46). Then fasten the board with the hollow side down and carve off the mass of the wood from the bottom with a large gouge and the mallet (Illus. 46). Thereafter, finish with chisel and flat gouge.

There are only a few basic forms for bowls and plates. Base your work on these and—in any case—do not imitate turnery. Carved and turned bowls each have their own characteristics.

Carving bowls is an excellent exercise to prepare for sculpturing in wood. You learn to make larger objects and to carve deeper into the wood. The illustrated bowls and candlesticks may induce you to experiment further with creating in wood.

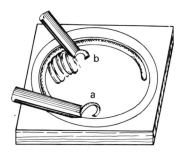 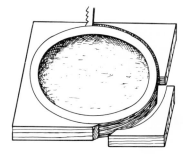 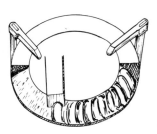

Illus. 46. Carve trench (a); hollow out bowl (b). Saw hollowed form from block, clamp upside down, shape bottom.

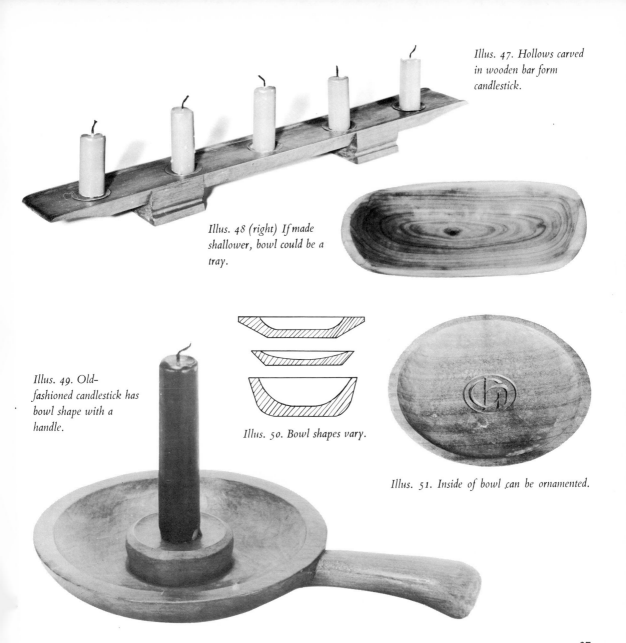

Illus. 47. Hollows carved in wooden bar form candlestick.

Illus. 48 (right) If made shallower, bowl could be a tray.

Illus. 49. Old-fashioned candlestick has bowl shape with a handle.

Illus. 50. Bowl shapes vary.

Illus. 51. Inside of bowl can be ornamented.

Relief Carving

Relief is the transition from two-dimensional drawing to three-dimensional sculpture. The third dimension, depth, in relief is only a fraction of that in reality. A head which might have a depth of some 8 inches in reality may appear with a depth of perhaps 1 inch on a relief. This should be kept in mind; the forms must be kept relatively flat.

Another essential in carving relief is to show as much "broadsides" as possible—the head from the side, the breasts in front view, etc. As the relief must remain attached to the background, as much as possible of the original, wooden frontal surface is retained.

In simple reliefs, human figures and animals should move *along* the front (Illus. 52) and not emerge from the background, striding *toward* the front. A head in relief should be rounded but not so much that it looks like a halved sphere. A relief may be either low (bas-relief), as we have been discussing, or high (haut-relief), where the figures project further from the background and a more complex design is possible.

To carve a relief, you again start by drawing the design on the wood. Then you cleanly define the contour lines and carve out the background, as you did with your carving of ornaments. Carefully carve the various forms, frequently taking a critical look at your work. The best method of working is to clamp your board vertically, so that you can judge how it will look when it is finished and hanging on a wall.

Illus. 52. Note that all the figures move across the front and are attached to the background instead of jutting from it.

Sculpture - Clamping the Wood

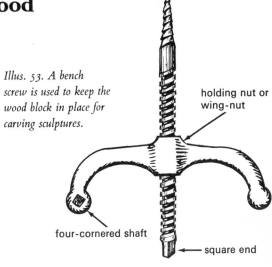

Illus. 53. A bench screw is used to keep the wood block in place for carving sculptures.

holding nut or wing-nut

four-cornered shaft

square end

While relief work is meant to be viewed from the front and requires a plank only an inch or two in thickness, sculpture in the round is meant to be viewed from all sides and requires a large block of wood. This presents the problem of holding the block securely while you work on it with gouges and mallet. One effective method is to use a bench screw (Illus. 53).

First drill a hole in the base of the block. Screw the pointed end of the bench screw into the hole, which should be the diameter of the screw's shank and not of the threads. Then the free part of the screw (with the wing-nut removed) is pushed from above through a hole either in the worktable or in a horizontal block of wood clamped to the worktable (Illus. 54). If you use the worktable itself add a drilled block of wood beneath it. Then secure the bench screw tightly with the wing-nut.

The long bench screw cannot be used with some pieces. In those cases, a larger board is fixed to the bottom of the carving block with wood screws and this board is attached to the worktable with clamps.

Other aids, such as a wood worker's vise and a swivel vise are available.

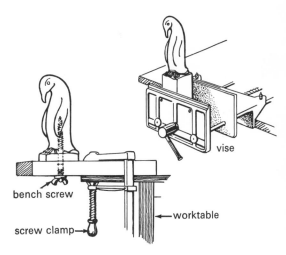

vise

bench screw

screw clamp

worktable

Illus. 54. Bench screw in position, or vise, holds work.

Animal Sculpture

Zoos and farms give you the occasion to study animals. First carve an animal which has a very simple form. A fish or a bird is easier to carve than a horse or a tiger. Whether you start by making a model in plaster or by making a simple sketch is a matter of your intention and of your experience.

After you have decided on the size, you draw the main view on the block of wood. If you are using a small block of wood, you can now saw out the contour with a coping saw or fret saw. (For larger pieces, rough out the form with a crosscut and a ripsaw.) Now you have an animal figure similar to a toy (Illus. 55). By rasping and polishing its edges, you have already produced a simple animal sculpture. But you want to make something better, so now carve out more of the wood with chisel and gouge.

For blocking out initial masses, you start by using a fairly large gouge, which you drive with a mallet. As carving progresses, flat chisels and smaller gouges are used. The tools become finer and, if you use a mallet, your stroke becomes lighter. For this type of work, you will often use your bent gouges, as there are more deep-lying parts. The surface is finished with a flat gouge and the diagonal chisel. Whether you finish with large or small carving cuts on the surface is a matter of taste. Formerly, a rough surface was preferred; nowadays surfaces are often polished, leaving no traces of the cuts.

Illus. 55. Saw the contour of a horse from a block of wood. Some work with gouges and chisels transforms the cut-out.

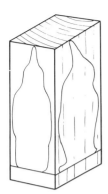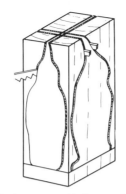

Illus. 56. Draw front and side views on block; saw along contours to pedestal; cut away excess wood; then carve.

Certain small forms allow you to saw the block from all four sides instead of sawing one contour as in the previous project. The front and side views are drawn on the block (Illus. 56). Then you saw along the drawn lines with the coping saw, but do not saw farther than the pedestal. This is done to leave a firm base. At the top, place a small peg in the saw cut. The superfluous wood at the bottom is carved off after the four sawings have been completed. This is the way a cabinetmaker manufactures curved furniture legs.

Now carving this sculpture is not very difficult because the main points had been fixed and part of the contour lines have been made by the sawing. This type of work can sometimes be completed with a sharp pocketknife only. You hold the workpiece in your left hand and turn it, while you carve with your right.

Illus. 57. First penguin is one diagrammed above; other two are variations.

Illus. 58. Figures
that cannot be
sawed along
contours must be
blocked out, then
carved in detail, as
these bear cubs.

The group of cubs (Illus. 58) is more difficult. If you look carefully at the illustration, you will recognize in the finished work the rectangular block of wood from which it has been carved. Sawing is not of much help in this case. You draw the outlines and the main forms on the block and, starting from the top, you carve the shoulders and the front legs. The outlines gradually emerge. Use your calipers and compass to check the size and depth of the parts. An experienced wood carver blocks out little and initially lets some of the superfluous wood stay in place. In this way, the shapes can still be altered somewhat as you work.

After all the sides have been well carved, you start with the details—the toes, ears and eyes; and you finish with fine, careful cuts. This group of cubs has not been polished; the shaggy pelt has been indicated by a few cuts.

The fox (Illus. 59) has been carved in mahogany, leaving out all details. This piece expresses strength and energy.

If you do decide to work from a clay or plaster model, consult the chapter on transferring measurements by punctuating devices.

Illus. 59. Leaving
out details, as in
this fox, can add
power to the form.

32

Illus. 60. Both the cat and the seal pictured here are simplified forms, with the wood smoothed to a fine finish. The grain on the seal is appropriate to the animal's pose, while the cat's stance requires no special grain pattern.

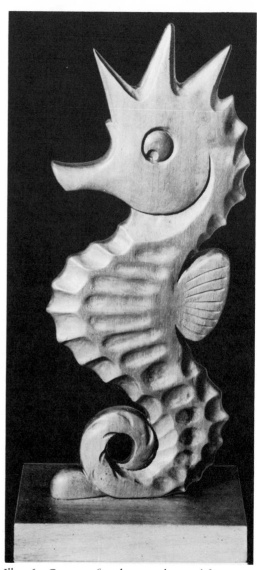

Illus. 61. Straight grain flows with bowed head of penguin.

Illus. 62. Contours of sea horse can be sawed first.

34

The Figure

There is no uniform opinion on the relative merits of carving directly in the wood or utilizing a clay model. Both techniques have been used by great artists, some working directly in wood or stone and others first making a wax or clay model.

During the so-called archaic period, the ancient Greeks worked directly in stone. These sculptures are like pillars, with the arms kept close to the body. The sculptors from that period blocked out the superfluous material of a rectangular block from all four sides in layers. When the Greek sculptors in later times made more dynamic works, they also made clay and wax models and worked with casts of plaster.

Working with or without a model depends not only on the talent and experience of the sculptor, but on the subject itself. A small simple piece is often carved without a preliminary model. Large and dynamic pieces are made with models, even by experienced artists.

The principles of animal sculpture apply to carving figures as well. With small and medium-sized pieces, the contour lines are sawed out. For the initial carving, details are neglected while you concentrate on larger planes and main lines. The work should be clamped in an upright position as the total effect can be better judged this way. Carving the details is done only after the total composition has been correctly carved.

A symmetrical figure is easier to carve than a dynamic subject. You start with the points of the front which stick out most. (For instance, the elbows of the sculpture on the cover.) After measuring with your compass or calipers, you carve more deeply, looking for further main fixing-points. In the roughed-out form of the

Illus. 63. Symmetrical figures are easier to carve than dynamic ones (Illus. 1).

35

Illus. 64. Front and side views are carved first. Same steps are followed as for animal sculpture. Here the background was left on to show relationship of carving in the round to relief.

| drawn on block | initial carving | finished work |

flute player (Illus. 64), the hands, the face, body and feet are only indicated. The background is left on so you can see the relationship to relief carving. The contour of the front is of special importance. The side views are done only after the main parts of the front and the contour lines have been correctly made. Check to see that all the important points have been fixed deeply enough in the block; points, for instance, like the shoulders, hands and forehead.

After the sides, carve the back. It is not necessary, however, to adhere strictly to this sequence of stages in carving. It is much more important to concentrate on the total view, the composition. You may very well "go over" your piece several times in succession, carving the front, the sides and the back. Gradually, you will "peel out" your work, leaving the details to the last stage.

For large pieces of sculpture, it is a good idea to hollow out the inside to prevent cracking. Information on how to do this is given in the chapter on puppets.

Puppet Heads

Making puppet heads is good preparation for sculpturing portrait busts in wood. Start by making some sketches of the size and expression of various faces. For carving, use a light-colored wood.

Draw the profile on the block, fixing the position of the point of the nose. At this point drill a hole and insert a thin peg or dowel to prevent a long nose from chipping off. The dotted lines in Illus. 65 show the peg and the saw cuts. Now you start carving, going deeply into the block but leaving the nose sticking out. Indicate the forehead, eye sockets, mouth and chin. Then carve the sides, often with large ears, and conclude with the back of the head.

Before carving the finished details, first make the head hollow. This is to make it lighter to handle when in use.

Separate the head in two parts behind the ears. With most woods, this can be done by splitting; take a large chisel or a hatchet and drive it with a sharp blow of a wooden mallet. You can also saw the head in half. As an alternative, you can start with two separate blocks and join them with wood-cement before carving. In that case, place a sheet of paper between both halves when cementing them together, so you will know exactly where to split open the cement seams after your initial carving.

After hollowing out both halves, cement them back together again and finish your carving with details. Make certain you have hollowed out a hole in the neck for the finger of the puppeteer. The puppet's facial expression can be enhanced by painting.

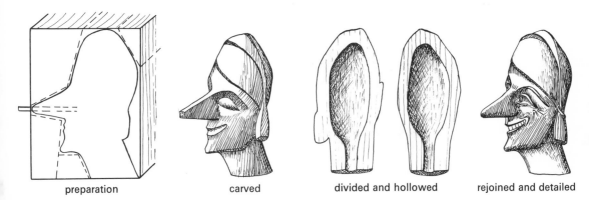

preparation   carved   divided and hollowed   rejoined and detailed

Illus. 65. Draw profile on block, insert peg, saw out form. Carve face. Split and hollow carving. Cement carving back.

Sculpturing Portraits in Wood

To sculpture a portrait, you need a life-size model of your subject in plaster or oil-based clay called plasticine or plastilene. Using clay saves you the work of casting the plaster. Start with the points which are most projected: the tip of the nose, the forehead, the mouth and chin. Carve deeply to fix the eyes, the jaws and the temples. If you have no experience, you will have a tendency to make faces too flat, so study the side views of the face as well as the front view, and check your observations by measuring.

Details are carved after all main forms, total height and width, as well as the profile are correct. Striking heads with strong features are easier to carve than heads

Illus. 66b. To begin, block out the masses as usual.

of children; a portrait in relief is easier than a three-dimensional portrait.

Only a minority of sculptors carve portraits directly from nature and they have great talent and long experience. Most portrait busts are made by first making a plaster or clay model and then transferring this to the wood with the aid of calipers or a punctuating device. For heads with strong features, you can use oak or American walnut; for children's heads use basswood.

Illus. 66a. Use a clay model of your subject as a guide.

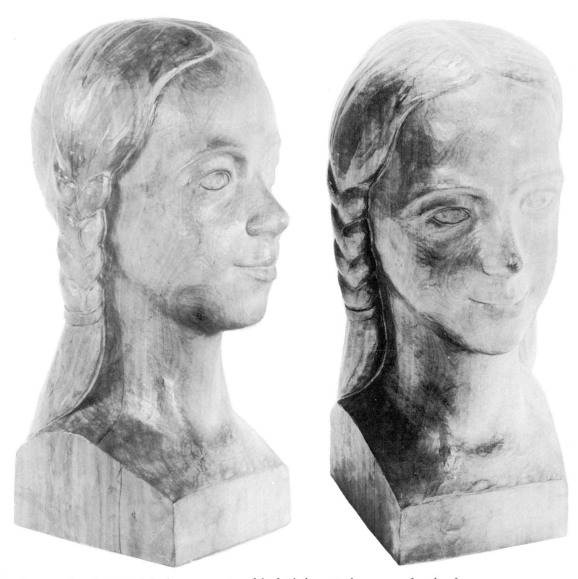

Illus. 67. The side view and the three-quarter view of the finished portrait show a many-faceted surface.

Punctuating or Pointing Up

Punctuating is transferring the measurements of the clay or plaster model point by point to wood or stone. This can be done in many different ways and the ancient Greeks knew various punctuating systems 2,000 years ago.

The usual punctuating device consists of a brass cross-work with three pins and a movable series of rods with a measuring needle (Illus. 68).

The top pin is hung from the top of the model and the two horizontal pins are positioned so they touch the base of the model (Illus. 69). These are the three main points from which all others are measured. Move the device to the wooden block you are going to carve and mark off these points. With the device returned to the model, place the measuring needle on the model at its furthest protruding point. Now you can start punctuating.

First transfer the protruding points (forehead, nose, chin) and then the lower lying ones. Make a small cross to mark each transferred point on the model and bore into your wood with a fluting tool or a drill until the needle can be pushed to the right depth. Here, also make a mark with a pencil. However, do not push the needle all the way in. Leave a thin layer of extra wood, which you will later carve away during the finishing. Beginners especially must take care not to fix the points too deeply at the start. After the first marks are made you carve the rough form and repeat the pointing process. You may point and carve as many times as necessary. All marks remain as small elevations until you finish your work.

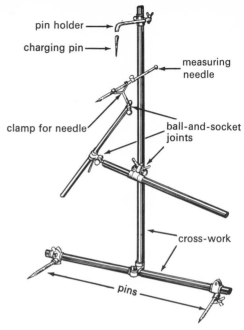

Illus. 68. A punctuating device pinpoints protrusions, etc., for transferring measurements from clay to wood.

You can construct the punctuating device shown on page 42 yourself. The triangle is made of wood or of metal. The three pointed legs take the place of the cross-work. A wooden bar of corresponding length is slotted to hold the pointed end of a ruler, which is held in position by the two sides of the slot. The bar is clamped to the triangle with a small clamp or a clothespin and the point of the ruler is placed on the points to be fixed. You can read the depth at which you must fix the points on your wood from the ruler. For some types of work, you may prefer a square frame instead of a triangular one.

Illus. 69. The three pins remain in their positions while you move the measuring needle to fix the points. At the right is the finished work in wood.

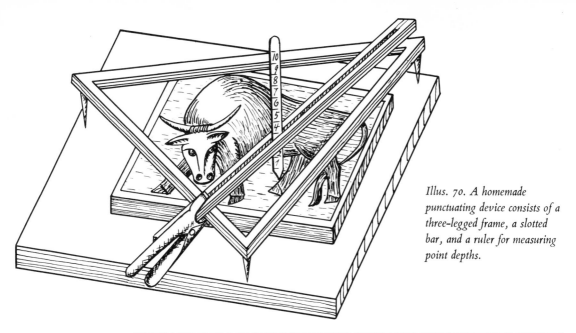

Illus. 70. A homemade punctuating device consists of a three-legged frame, a slotted bar, and a ruler for measuring point depths.

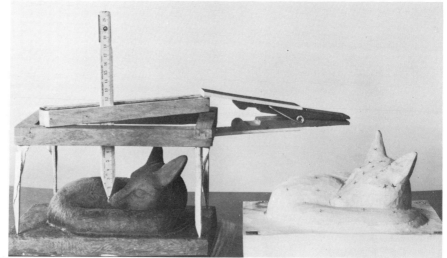

Illus. 71. A four-legged frame may be used as well. Crosses on wooden fox indicate where points have been measured. Finished sculpture is on page 43.

Surface Finishing

Good wood carving can be spoiled by bad finishing. Therefore, first practice on scraps of wood or leave this work to an expert. The workshop should be warm and dry. Humid and cold air is detrimental to this work.

First of all, you can repair spots that have been damaged by the pressure of clamps by moistening them. If the slight hollows do not disappear, you can make the moisture penetrate better into the wood by making some pinpricks and moistening again. This will cause the compressed part of the wood to swell. Cracks and holes are best filled with plastic wood, which you can purchase in various colors and which can be mixed. It can be thinned with cellulose thinner. Minute cracks are filled with colored wax.

Waxing is an old and simple way to give a beautiful matte sheen to wood carving. Dissolve grated beeswax in turpentine—about 1 ounce of wax in $\frac{1}{2}$ pint of turpentine. Let the solution stand during one night and, after stirring it, apply thinly with a brush. When the surface is dry go over it with a soft brush. For wood with large pores this treatment should be repeated. Instead of beeswax, you may also use prepared paste wax or furniture wax. Wax closes the pores of the wood and protects against dirt and dust. Unfortunately, a coating of wax is not water-resistant.

Illus. 72. A good finish, like the matte sheen on this fox, enriches the artistic effect of the sculpture.

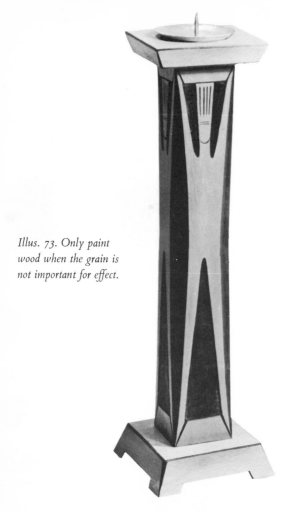

*Illus. 73. Only paint
wood when the grain is
not important for effect.*

A matte finish with cellulose lacquer results in a water-repellent and scratch-proof surface. Stained and coarse-pored woods should first be treated with cellulose wood-filler. After that is dry, you may apply the lacquer. For smooth surfaces, a wad of cotton and nettle cloth is

better than a brush. Matting with lacquer gives a silky gloss. If the coating is too thick, a greasy looking surface will result. Therefore, do not apply too much lacquer and polish the surface with a clean cloth after it is dry. The lacquer may make the surface somewhat coarse. In that case, carefully finish the work with very fine sandpaper and apply some more diluted lacquer. You can dilute and clean your brush with lacquer-thinner. The color and grain of the wood are preserved when you use lacquer.

Linseed oil is also used to enhance the grain pattern of the wood carving. The contrast between light and dark streaks is stressed especially with walnut, cherry and oak. After the linseed oil has dried well, you may in addition apply a coating of wax or a matte oil-varnish.

Light-colored woods may be stained to imitate other woods. Spirit vehicles penetrate well, but have the disadvantage of making soft wood darker than you intend. Water vehicles also penetrate excellently, but they raise the grain of the wood, which then has to be smoothed.

Before staining, the wood is first soaked in water. When the surfaces are dry, they are carefully smoothed with pumice or emery and the wood particles are brushed off. Then the wood is soaked again before the staining solution is applied to the wet wood. End grain must be thoroughly soaked to prevent it from absorbing too much of the solution and darkening more than the other wood. Besides water vehicles, there are several types of chemical vehicles you can investigate.

Painting covers bad and dark spots in the wood, but the beautiful grain patterns and the natural color of the wood are covered as well. Therefore, painting should be considered only if the sculptures are to be seen from a distance, for instance statues in churches. These mostly stand in shadow and often need color to be seen well. Painted wood that is exposed to the weather is often coated with a colorless outer varnish.

Modern Wood Carving

Essentially, there is less difference between modern and "traditional" art than it would at first appear. Artists have never exactly copied nature; that was not their intention. Abstract art is nothing new; it is found in all periods of history, and abstract drawings were the origin for Chinese and for Egyptian alphabet characters.

The wood carver should follow his own taste. The following illustrations show how varied wood carvings can be. The first hare shows details, like eyes and teeth. The other one omits details but shows which animal inspired the artist. Also, this piece shows more of the structure of the wood. The third sculpture is clearly an animal—it has a head and legs—but you cannot recognize a specific type of animal. It could be a symbol for all four-legged animals. The last illustrations are abstract and geometrical.

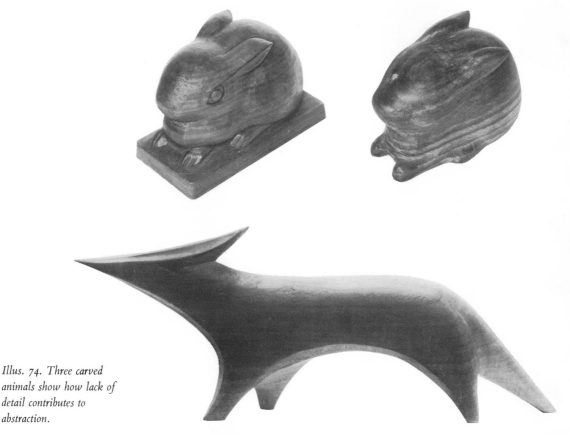

Illus. 74. Three carved animals show how lack of detail contributes to abstraction.

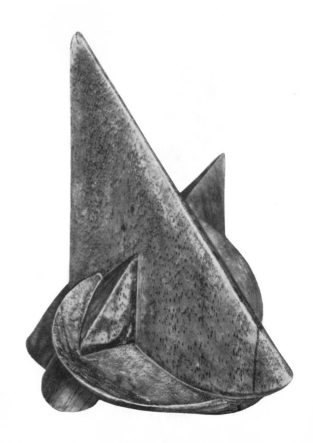

Illus. 75. These works are purely abstract, being based solely on geometrical forms.

Artistic Results

When designing your work, you should consider not only the characteristics of the particular wood you will use but also your intended *manner* of working. Are you going to polish the work with fine sandpaper or do you intend to show the last cuts made by your tools? One wood carver may carefully stress small cuts, while another may use strong, large cuts. These personal touches are lost by rasping, filing and polishing. On the other hand, smoothing techniques expose the structure and beauty of the wood. The choice of technique is decided by the wood carver in view of his material and the results he desires.

Compare the smoothness of the figure in Illus. 1 with the many-faceted surface of the portrait in Illus. 67, page 39.

Though, in modern times, wood carving has been increasingly superseded by mass-produced utensils, the creation of wooden objects and their ornamenting by carving has always been part of civilization. Carved panels from tombs have been preserved from the old Egyptian civilization of 4,000 years ago. The Romans followed Greek examples to make precious furniture for a rich, upper class. Wood carving and wood sculpture flourished in Europe in the Middle Ages, when the cathedrals were adorned with statues.

Later, during the Renaissance, Baroque, and Rococo periods, wood carvers worked not only for the Church, but also for princes and rich merchants, for guilds and town halls. Authorities and churches still commission the works of wood carvers, and many great sculptors, like England's Henry Moore, prefer wood as a material

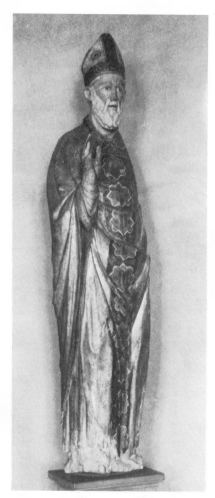

Illus. 76. Gilded bishop is 14th-century Italian work.

for their works. The more you work with wood, the more you will feel yourself a part of the fine tradition of wood carving, and perhaps contribute to it. This book is meant to inspire and guide you toward that aim.

Index